US COAST GUARD
EQUIPMENT AND VEHICLES

BY MARTHA LONDON

CONTENT CONSULTANT
CAPTAIN R. B. WATTS, PhD
US COAST GUARD (RETIRED)

Kids Core

An Imprint of Abdo Publishing
abdobooks.com

abdobooks.com

Printed in the United States of America, North Mankato, Minnesota
052021
092021

THIS BOOK CONTAINS
RECYCLED MATERIALS

Cover Photo: Petty Officer 3rd Class Ross Ruddell/US Coast Guard
Interior Photos: Petty Officer 3rd Class George Degener/US Coast Guard/Defense Visual Information Distribution Service, 4–5; Ensign Justin Z. Strassfield/US Coast Guard/Defense Visual Information Distribution Service, 6; Hulton Archive/Archive Photos/Getty Images, 9; Petty Officer 1st Class Sara Muir/US Coast Guard/Defense Visual Information Distribution Service, 10; Petty Officer 1st Class Fred Sullivan/US Coast Guard, 12–13; Petty Officer 1st Class Rob Simpson/US Coast Guard, 15; Chief Petty Officer Lauren Jorgensen/US Coast Guard/Defense Visual Information Distribution Service, 16; Petty Officer 3rd Class Corinne Zilnicki/US Coast Guard/Defense Visual Information Distribution Service, 18; Don Emmert/AFP/Getty Images, 20–21; Petty Officer 2nd Class Anthony Soto/US Coast Guard/Defense Visual Information Distribution Service, 22, 28; Petty Officer 1st Class Levi Read/US Coast Guard/Defense Visual Distribution Service, 25; Petty Officer 2nd Class Richard Brahm/US Coast Guard/ Defense Visual Information Distribution Service, 26, 29 (top); Petty Officer 1st Class Nick Ameen/US Coast Guard/Defense Visual Information Distribution Service, 29 (bottom)

Editor: Katharine Hale
Series Designer: Jake Nordby

Library of Congress Control Number: 2020948456

Publisher's Cataloging-in-Publication Data

Names: London, Martha, author.
Title: US Coast Guard equipment and vehicles / by Martha London
Description: Minneapolis, Minnesota : Abdo Publishing, 2022 | Series: US military equipment and vehicles | Includes online resources and index.
Identifiers: ISBN 9781532195457 (lib. bdg.) | ISBN 9781644946183 (pbk.) | ISBN 9781098215767 (ebook)
Subjects: LCSH: Coastal surveillance--Juvenile literature. | Sea-power--Juvenile literature. | Vehicles, Military--Juvenile literature. | Military supplies--Juvenile literature. | Military paraphernalia--Juvenile literature.
Classification: DDC 623.7--dc23

CONTENTS

CHAPTER 1
Protecting US Waters 4

CHAPTER 2
Equipment 12

CHAPTER 3
Vehicles 20

Important Gear 28
Glossary 30
Online Resources 31
Learn More 31
Index 32
About the Author 32

The USCGC *Alder* is based in Duluth, Minnesota. But it sometimes travels as far as the Canadian Arctic.

ALDER

U. S. COAST GUARD

CHAPTER **1**

PROTECTING US WATERS

A ship cruises across the lake. The ship belongs to the US Coast Guard. The ship's crew looks for dangers in the water. They also look for damaged **buoys** and signs. These show boaters where water is **shallow**. They also show when to move slowly.

The coast guard is responsible for changing buoys seasonally.

One buoy is cracked. The crew lifts the cracked buoy out of the water. There is a sandbar nearby. The buoy tells boats to steer away from the area. If the buoy had filled with water, it would have sunk. Boats could have gotten stuck on the sandbar.

The coast guard must also swap buoys out seasonally. Areas that get icy have summer buoys and winter buoys. Ice can freeze on top of summer buoys. This can make the buoy sink. Winter buoys are designed to resist the ice. The buoy can still show boaters where it is safe to go. The coast guard swaps summer and winter buoys twice a year.

Coast guard members do more than just deal with buoys. They keep the waters safe. They work hard to make sure ships and boats can reach docks safely. The coast guard also makes sure ships do not carry illegal drugs or weapons.

About the Coast Guard

Alexander Hamilton created the US Coast Guard in 1790. Ships called cutters patrolled the US coast. Crew members made sure traders paid taxes on the goods they were bringing into the country.

Over time, the coast guard grew. Crews worked on both coasts of the United States. Others worked on lakes and rivers.

A Small Group

The coast guard is one of the smallest branches of the military. There were 40,000 active duty members in the first half of 2020. Other branches are much larger. The US Marine Corps had 186,000 active marines at about the same time.

Alexander Hamilton was one of the Founding Fathers of the United States.

The US Coast Guard has many **duties** that are not related to war. The coast guard cares for lighthouses. Lighthouses alert boats and ships of shallow water. In icy waters, coast guard members warn other ships about icebergs. The coast guard also works to keep shores and waters clean.

Maintaining lighthouses and conducting search and rescue missions are among the many important duties of the coast guard.

The coast guard makes sure water is safe for boaters and swimmers. If people are in danger, the coast guard performs search and rescue missions. During wartime, the US Coast Guard works with the US Navy in the ocean. Coast guard members are always hard at work.

The coast guard retrieves sunken buoys. After one mission, a coast guard crew member wrote:

> After 30 minutes of playing the world's largest claw game we have our prize catch, and as responsible buoy fishermen we released a fully functioning and floating buoy immediately afterwards.

Source: Brandon Champion. "Coast Guard Ship Plays 'World's Largest Claw Game' to Get Sunken Buoy out of Lake Michigan." *MLive*, 3 Apr. 2020, mlive.com. Accessed 8 May 2020.

Comparing Texts

Does this quote support the information in this chapter? Or does it give a different perspective? Explain how in a few sentences.

The coast guard is responsible for rescuing people in bodies of water.

CHAPTER 2

EQUIPMENT

Coast guard members have many jobs. They use special equipment to keep them safe. Different jobs require different kinds of equipment.

Rescue Swimmers

Some coast guard members train to become rescue swimmers.

Rescue swimmers help people who are in danger in the water. Rescue swimmers wear a wet suit and a face mask. They swim out to help people. Sometimes rescue swimmers give a person a flotation device. Other times, swimmers carry the person to safety.

Wet suits are made of a thick material. It keeps swimmers warm. Rescue swimmers sometimes have to be in cold water. Or they have to be in the water for long periods of time. They wear wet suits so they do not become too cold.

Face masks are also important. Masks keep water out of a swimmer's eyes and nose. If swimmers have to dive under the surface of the water, they can still see.

A Rescue Swimmer's Equipment

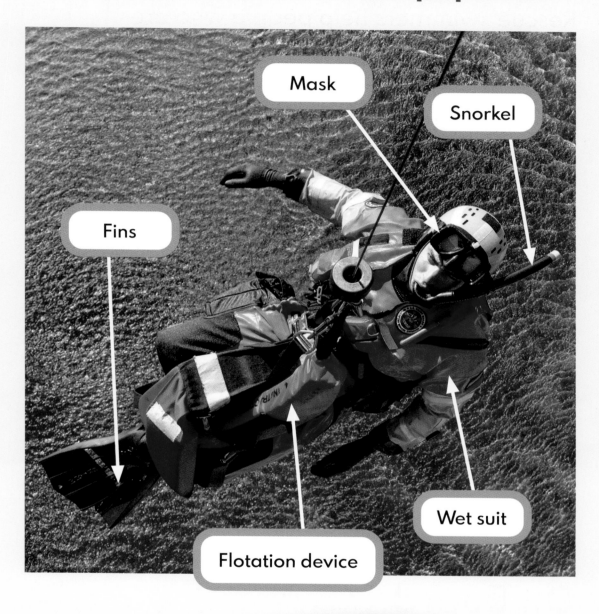

Mask

Snorkel

Fins

Wet suit

Flotation device

Snorkels help rescue swimmers breathe while swimming, and fins help them swim faster. All of this equipment helps rescue swimmers save lives.

The coast guard educates the public on the importance of life jackets.

On Board

Just like **civilians**, coast guard members wear life jackets when they are on their boats. Life jackets are important safety equipment.

They help people float. If coast guard members fall off the boat, a life jacket helps them stay above the water. They do not have to swim to stay above water. They can float and save energy until help arrives.

Cleaning Up after an Oil Spill

In April 2010, an oil rig exploded in the Gulf of Mexico. More than 210 million gallons (790 million L) of oil spilled into the ocean. The US Coast Guard led cleanup efforts. It worked to clean oil from the surface of the ocean. It also helped clean shorelines and wildlife.

Radios are essential to the work of the coast guard.

Coast guard members also have radios on their boats and ships. Radios allow a crew to communicate with boats that are in danger. If a crew needs to help a boat, they use a radio to talk with the other boat's crew.

Coast guard crews also use radios to communicate with teams on land. They can call for help if more guard members are needed for a job. Crews also talk to teams on land after a mission. They let everyone know they are safe.

Explore Online

Visit the website below. Does it give any new information about life jackets that wasn't in Chapter Two?

Life Jacket Safety Saves Lives

abdocorelibrary.com/coast-guard -equipment-vehicles

The USCGC *Eagle* is a tall ship. It is the only ship with sails active in the US military.

CHAPTER 3

VEHICLES

The US Coast Guard works on the water and in the air. It uses ships, boats, and helicopters. Coast guard members can quickly reach people and boats in need.

The USCGC *Hamilton* is a national security cutter based in Charleston, South Carolina.

On the Water

The US Coast Guard uses many different types of watercraft. Some are huge ships. Others are smaller boats. Coast guard members use ships and boats for different jobs. Both types of water vehicles are important.

A cutter is a type of ship. Any ship more than 65 feet (20 m) long is considered a cutter. The US Coast Guard has used cutters throughout its history. Cutters patrol the ocean and the Great Lakes. One type of cutter is the national security cutter. It is 418 feet (127 m) long. Its crew can board other boats or ships to search them for dangerous items. The coast guard is responsible for making sure people do not bring illegal items to the United States.

Protection from Pirates

One of the first jobs of the coast guard was to protect the United States against pirates. The coast guard used cutters. Cutters were faster than larger **passenger** ships. Crews chased pirate ships. Sometimes they pushed ships toward shore. Crews used their ships to make pirate ships crash. Today, the coast guard works with the US Navy to fight against pirates.

The coast guard uses smaller boats on lakes and rivers. These include Motor Life Boats (MLBs) and Response Boats. These boats can get into tight spaces. A small crew drives the boat. These boats can operate in shallow water. The sides of the boat are closer to the surface of the water. Swimmers and boaters in danger can be rescued more easily. Crew members can pull the people out of the water and onto the boat.

In the Air

Coast guard crews also fly helicopters. Helicopters can reach ships and boats that are far from shore quickly. One helicopter the US Coast Guard uses is the MH-65 Dolphin.

If a 47-foot (14-m) MLB is knocked over by a wave, it can right itself in 30 seconds.

The MH-65 Dolphin's top speed is 200 miles per hour (320 km/h).

A helicopter crew can find people more easily in open water. They can see a lot of area from the air. Helicopters are also faster than ships. When people are injured, the crew takes them directly to a hospital. Many large hospitals have a helicopter pad. Without helicopters, it would take much longer for people to get medical care.

The US Coast Guard has many duties. Members use equipment and vehicles to keep US waters safe. They also keep people safe on and off the water.

Further Evidence

Look at the website below. Does it give any new evidence to support Chapter Three?

Can a Boat Be a Life Saver?

abdocorelibrary.com/coast-guard -equipment-vehicles

IMPORTANT GEAR

National Security Cutter

- 418-foot (127-m) long ship
- Has a large crew
- Used to execute important missions concerning homeland security

753

U.S. COAST GUARD

MH-65 Dolphin

- Helicopter
- Used to search for boats or people
- Brings people to safety

Life Jackets

- Worn by coast guard members on boats
- Help crew members float if they fall overboard

Glossary

buoys
floating objects that tell swimmers and boats where the water is not safe

civilians
people who are not in the military

duties
responsibilities that are part of a job

oil rig
a machine that can extract oil from the ground

passenger
a person traveling on a boat, ship, or other vehicle

patrolled
watched for danger

shallow
not deep

Online Resources

To learn more about US Coast Guard equipment and vehicles, visit our free resource websites below.

Visit **abdocorelibrary.com** or scan this QR code for free Common Core resources for teachers and students, including vetted activities, multimedia, and booklinks, for deeper subject comprehension.

Visit **abdobooklinks.com** or scan this QR code for free additional online weblinks for further learning. These links are routinely monitored and updated to provide the most current information available.

Learn More

Abdo, Kenny. *United States Coast Guard*. Abdo Publishing, 2019.

London, Martha. *Military Ships*. Abdo Publishing, 2020.

Index

buoys, 5–7, 11

cutters, 8, 22–23

drugs, 7, 23

Hamilton, Alexander, 8

life jackets, 16–17
lighthouses, 9

Marine Corps, US, 8
MH-65 Dolphin, 24–27
Motor Life Boats (MLBs), 24

national security cutters, 23
Navy, US, 10, 23

oil spills, 17

pirates, 23

radios, 18–19
rescue swimmers, 13–14, 15

weapons, 7, 23
wet suits, 14, 15

About the Author

Martha London is a writer and educator. When she isn't writing, you can find her fishing, swimming, or canoeing on lakes and rivers.